What a Country!

Contents

A Century of Change   4

1901–1910: An Age of Hope   6

1911–1920: A Time of Trouble   8

1921–1930: Roaring Twenties   10

1931–1940: Hard Years   12

1941–1950: The War Years   14

1951–1960: Happier Days   16

1961–1970: Rights and Protests   18

1971–1980: A Decade of Doubt   20

1981–1990: Rich Rewards   22

1991–2000: You've Got Mail!   24

Going Forward   26

Game of the Century   28

Glossary   30

Index   31

Research Starters   32

Features

MY DIARY

If your father was away at war, what would you write in a letter to him? Read one child's letter during World War II on page 15.

IN THE NEWS

Read the front-page story around the world in July 1969 in **Man on Moon!** on page 19.

WORD BUILDER

Have you ever heard the word *yuppie*? Find out what this word stands for on page 23.

TIME LINK

Discover interesting facts in the **Game of the Century** on page 28.

SITESEEING • ART & ENTERTAINMENT

What did people enjoy doing in the 1950s?

Visit www.rigbyinfoquest.com

for more about ENTERTAINMENT.

A Century of Change

The twentieth century (1901–2000) was a time of tremendous change. During this time, amazing advances in science, medicine, and technology dramatically changed the way people lived, more than at any other time. From the first airplane flight to astronauts in space, from the invention of the radio to the computer age, humans made giant leaps forward. By the end of the century, many people in the Western world led longer and more comfortable lives.

Not everyone benefited from these changes, however. Many countries and people remained poor. New technology meant larger wars were fought in ways never seen before. These wars reshaped nations and changed the way that people thought about the world and its future.

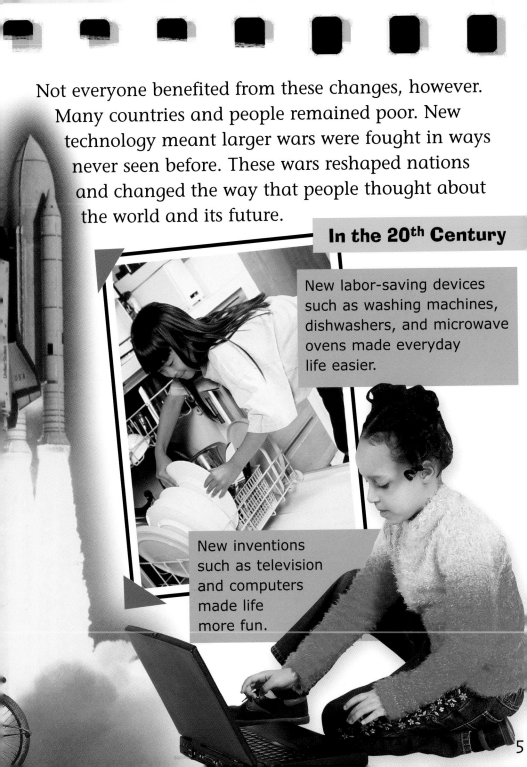

In the 20th Century

New labor-saving devices such as washing machines, dishwashers, and microwave ovens made everyday life easier.

New inventions such as television and computers made life more fun.

1901–1910: An Age of Hope

The century began full of hope. Many people moved from Europe to start new lives in countries such as the United States, Canada, Australia, and New Zealand. Others moved from the countryside to the cities and began jobs in industry. Exciting new industries were starting up in many Western nations, and cities were growing quickly.

During this decade, the Wright brothers made the first airplane and Henry Ford made the first affordable motorcar. Electricity lit up homes, and the first radio broadcast was made across the Atlantic Ocean. It was a time of peace and progress for much of the Western world.

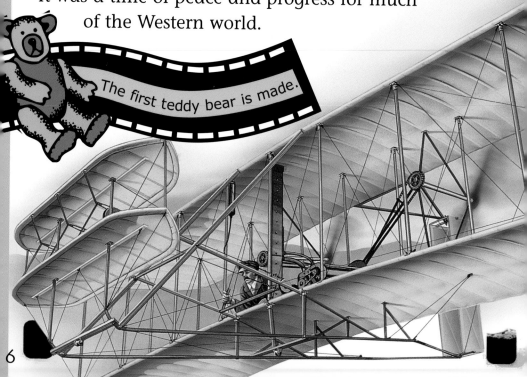

The first teddy bear is made.

The Wright Stuff

On December 17, 1903, Orville Wright made the first powered flight near Kitty Hawk, North Carolina. He and his brother Wilbur had spent years designing the gasoline-engined *Flyer* in Dayton, Ohio. At first, people thought that "flying machines" were just a fad. They said that the invention was nothing more than a costly toy.

The Wright brothers' airplane, *Flyer*

Henry Ford invented the first mass-produced motorcar, the Model *T*, in 1908.

1911–1920: A Time of Trouble

Peace didn't last for long. In Europe, dangerous **alliances** between nations led to the start of a huge war there in 1914. This war was like no other one before. It was the first global war. It involved soldiers from many different countries. Soldiers faced terrible modern weapons such as machine guns, tanks, and poison gas. The number of deaths was huge.

In the Trenches

Soldiers from both sides were forced to dig trenches into the earth to protect themselves from machine gunfire. Soon a line of trenches ran across Western Europe. Life in the trenches was muddy, cold, and terrifying. When the soldiers went "over the top" to attack, many were killed.

By the end of World War I, many of the old European empires were destroyed and new nations were created. In Russia, the first **communist** state was formed and named the Soviet Union.

ON HER THEIR LIVES DEPEND

WOMEN MUNITION WORKERS

Enrol at once

While men were away fighting, women took over their jobs in factories and offices and on farms. They proved they could work as well as any man. This helped people who were fighting for women's rights to vote. Although New Zealand was the first country to give women the vote in 1893, women in Britain did not win the right to vote until 1918. The United States gave women the right to vote two years later.

1921-1930: Roaring Twenties

The twenties were a time of celebration in many
Western countries. World War I was over and
businesses grew. Growing industries such as
car manufacturing created many new jobs. People
had plenty of money to spend and enjoyed free time.
They listened to jazz on the radio and danced the
Charleston and the foxtrot. Talking movies were
very popular, too.

During the twenties, many young women called flappers
bobbed their hair and danced the lively Charleston.
They were called flappers because of the way they
flapped their arms as they danced!

While countries in Europe were still struggling to recover from the war, the United States became the most important business power in the world. Americans kept on spending, but the good times could not last forever.

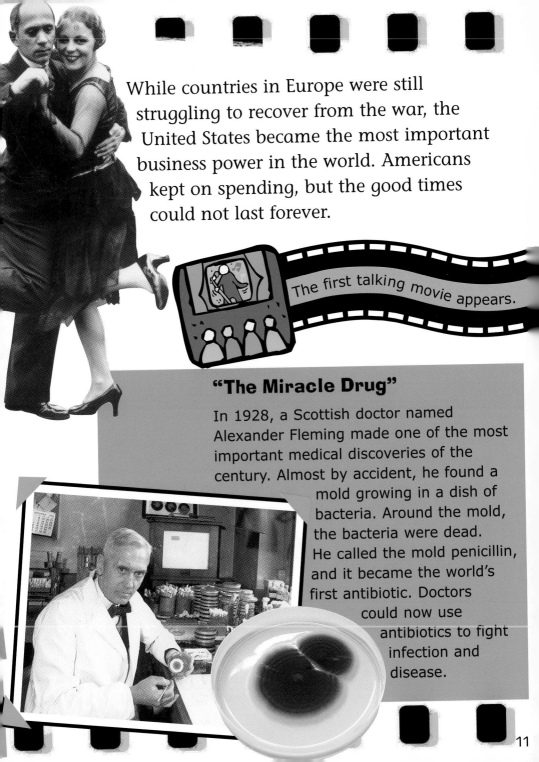

The first talking movie appears.

"The Miracle Drug"

In 1928, a Scottish doctor named Alexander Fleming made one of the most important medical discoveries of the century. Almost by accident, he found a mold growing in a dish of bacteria. Around the mold, the bacteria were dead. He called the mold penicillin, and it became the world's first antibiotic. Doctors could now use antibiotics to fight infection and disease.

1931-1940: Hard Years

In 1929, the New York **stock market** had crashed.
Banks and businesses closed down overnight.
Millions of people lost their savings and their jobs.
The crash caused a chain reaction around the world.
Unemployment and poverty spread. This time of hunger
and poverty was known as the Great Depression.

The first pinball machine is invented.

During the Great Depression, millions of jobless people stood in long breadlines. They waited for handouts of free food so they could feed their families.

Franklin D. Roosevelt

In 1932, Franklin D. Roosevelt was elected President of the United States. He set to work helping Americans and businesses. His **New Deal** gave food, shelter, and jobs to the unemployed. England, Canada, Australia, and New Zealand had similar programs. In Europe, however, some desperate countries became **dictatorships**. In Germany, a dictator named Adolf Hitler gained power.

Adolf Hitler was the head of the National Socialists (Nazis) in Germany. He won power by promising to solve Germany's problems. Once he was elected, he got rid of the **democratic** government and set up a dictatorship built on fear.

On September 1, 1939, Germany had invaded Poland. The Nazis quickly took control of most of Europe. Only Britain and her allies stood against the Germans. The United States did not want to get involved in another war, but when Japan attacked Pearl Harbor in 1941, America was forced to join the war.

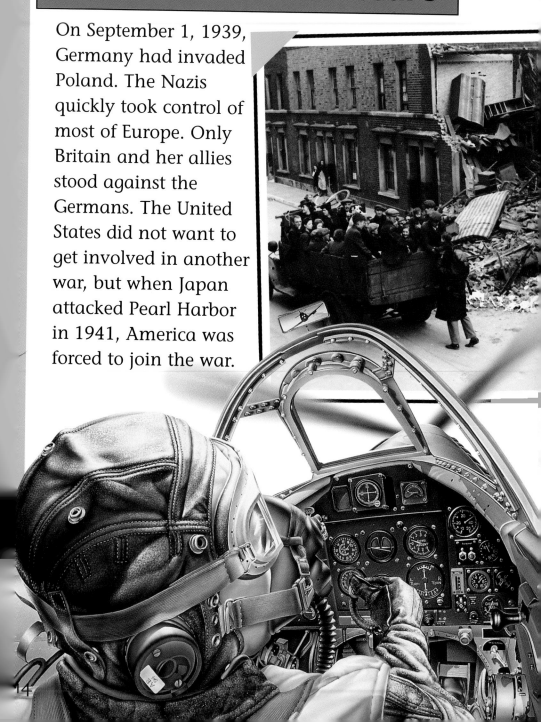

World War II was a global war. It touched everybody's lives. Other people as well as soldiers became the targets of bombs and air raids. When the war finally ended in 1945, Europe lay in ruins. Many millions of men, women, and children had lost their lives. A new organization called the **United Nations** was set up to try preventing such a war from ever happening again.

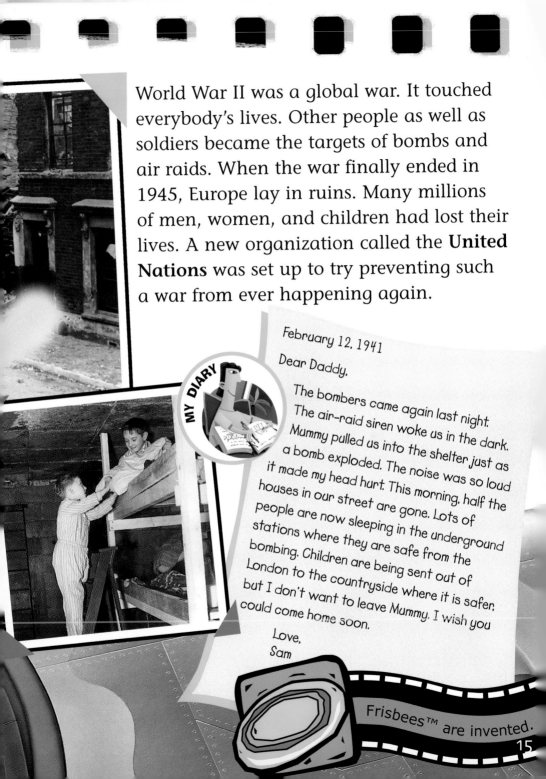

MY DIARY

February 12, 1941

Dear Daddy,

The bombers came again last night. The air-raid siren woke us in the dark. Mummy pulled us into the shelter just as a bomb exploded. The noise was so loud it made my head hurt. This morning, half the houses in our street are gone. Lots of people are now sleeping in the underground stations where they are safe from the bombing. Children are being sent out of London to the countryside where it is safer, but I don't want to leave Mummy. I wish you could come home soon.

Love,
Sam

Frisbees™ are invented.

1951–1960: Happier Days

After the war, the United States led the world in a period of good economy called a boom. Soldiers returning from the war married, and many babies were born. They were called the baby boomers. New communities and businesses grew, more people had jobs, and living was quite comfortable.

The first television broadcast took place in 1936, but it wasn't until the fifties that most people had a television in their homes.

What did people enjoy doing in the 1950s?
Visit **www.rigbyinfoquest.com**
for more about ENTERTAINMENT.

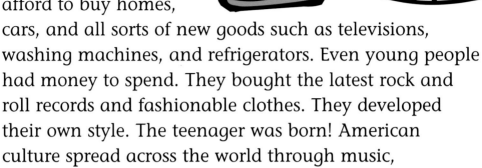

Many people could afford to buy homes, cars, and all sorts of new goods such as televisions, washing machines, and refrigerators. Even young people had money to spend. They bought the latest rock and roll records and fashionable clothes. They developed their own style. The teenager was born! American culture spread across the world through music, television, and movies.

Elvis Presley was called the King of Rock 'n' Roll. He took the world by storm with songs such as "Blue Suede Shoes" and "Heartbreak Hotel." Many adults were shocked by his performances, but most teenagers loved him!

17

1961-1970: Rights and Protests

Not everybody shared in the good times. In the United States, African Americans were often denied their **civil rights** and not treated fairly. Women and other groups were also sometimes treated unfairly. During the sixties, many people began to fight against these problems. One great civil rights leader was Martin Luther King. He believed that peaceful protest was the best way to bring about change.

Martin Luther King, Jr. (1929-1968)

In some states, African Americans were prevented from voting and separated from white people in schools and other public places. Martin Luther King, Jr., a Baptist minister, led peaceful marches and sit-ins to protest against these unjust laws.

In 1963, during a march in Washington, D.C., he made one of the greatest speeches of the century, beginning "I have a dream" and speaking of a world free from prejudice. The next year, the Civil Rights Act became law.

Meanwhile, some young people challenged the world of their parents. Young adults who wore their hair long and talked about the need for peace and love were called hippies. When the United States joined the war against Vietnam, some young men refused to fight. There were anti-war demonstrations around the world. The decade ended with excitement when an astronaut first walked on the moon.

IN THE NEWS

July 21, 1969

Man on Moon!

On July 20, 1969, at 4:17 P.M. Eastern Daylight Time, Neil Armstrong became the first man to walk on the Moon. He stepped off the ladder of the Lunar Module Eagle onto the moon's dusty surface. His first words were, "This is one small step for man, but one giant leap for mankind."

Remote-controlled toys are invented.

1971-1980: A Decade of Doubt

In the seventies, an **oil crisis** hit the world. People spent less and business slowed down. Unemployment increased and prices soared. For the first time, people saw that Earth's resources are limited and became concerned about the ways industries were harming the environment. Industries were polluting the air and water, and logging was destroying the forests. Many people joined groups such as Friends of the Earth and Greenpeace to help protect the environment.

As unemployment grew in the Western world, people lost confidence in their governments. Some young people expressed their anger in a new form of music called punk rock.

The first computer games are sold.

Earth Watch

On April 22, 1970, twenty million Americans marched through cities and towns across the nation to show they wanted a healthy, clean environment. Some children carried brooms to show they wanted to clean up the world. The first Earth Day led to the creation of the U.S. Environmental Protection Agency and the Clean Air, Clean Water, and Endangered Species acts.

1981-1990: Rich Rewards

The eighties were the decade of money. Governments encouraged business growth with tax cuts. Some people made lots of money, and some spent lots of money. While the rich got richer, however, the poor often got poorer. Developing countries struggled to pay off their debts. When drought struck parts of Africa, thousands of people faced starvation.

LIVE AID

Musicians from around the world came together to raise money to help starving people through Live Aid concerts.

Skateboarding becomes popular.

In Eastern Europe, the fall of the Berlin Wall separating East Germany from West Germany marked the end of communist rule. Many families there were reunited, and the world looked forward to a new era of peace.

In 1989, the East German government knocked down the Berlin Wall, which had divided the city of Berlin and the country of Germany for twenty-eight years.

WORD BUILDER

The term yuppie began in the eighties. "Yuppie" is an acronym. It stands for Young Urban Professionals. Yuppies earned lots of money and enjoyed spending it on luxuries such as fancy cars.

23

1991–2000: You've Got Mail!

The last decade of the twentieth century began with great hope. Nelson Mandela led the South African people to their first true democratic election. People in the new countries formed when the communist Soviet Union broke apart were now also freely electing leaders.

By the end of the 1990s, the world seemed a much smaller place. Many people could travel easily and quickly almost anywhere on Earth. They watched live global television and chatted on mobile phones. They owned their own computers and communicated worldwide on the Internet. Information and ideas were shared instantly. People gained a better understanding of other people and places. Technology had connected the world.

In 1995, the first movie to be created totally by computer animation was shown in movie theaters.

Nelson Mandela

Nelson Mandela was the leader of the African National Congress, a movement to stop apartheid in South Africa. Apartheid policy meant that blacks had to live apart from whites, had no right to vote, and were treated as second-class citizens. In 1964, Mandela was thrown into prison because the government did not like his ideas.

Finally, in 1990, President F. W. de Klerk released Mandela from prison. Together, they worked to establish true democracy and fairness in South Africa. Mandela was elected President of South Africa in 1994.

Going Forward

In the year 2000, people could look back on a century of great achievements. Despite two terrible world wars, many nations and people were learning to get along better. There was a greater respect for human rights. Organizations such as the United Nations helped to settle conflicts and assist poorer nations. There was a new understanding of the problems facing the environment and the poorer people of the world.

Many people now lead healthier, happier lives, thanks to the advances made during the twentieth century. The challenge for the twenty-first century is to see that these benefits are passed on to everyone.

The United Nations organizes deliveries of food and medical supplies to countries affected by drought or war.

Many changes could take place in the twenty-first century. We can only imagine what the world of the future will be like!

Game of the Century

START

1901

Take an extra turn.

Australia becomes self-governing

1903

Wright brothers make first successful airplane flight

Fly forward 3 spaces.

1914

Start again.

World War I begins in Europe

1918

World War I ends

Stay and celebrate. Miss a turn.

British women gain the right to vote

Girls move on 1 space.

1918

1920

U.S. women gain the right to vote

Boys move on 1 space.

1928

Penicillin, the first antibiotic, is discovered

1933

Hitler becomes leader of Germany

1932

F. D. Roosevelt elected president of U.S.A.

1931

Canada and New Zealand become independent

Send your opponent back 1 space.

Stock market crash starts Great Depression

Miss 2 turns.

1929

se Owens wins r gold medals the Olympics

Sprint forward 3 spaces.

1936

1939

World War II begins after Hitler invades Poland

Start again.

Japan bombs Pearl Harbor and U.S.A. enters war

Atomic bombs destroy Hiroshima and Nagasaki, ending World War II

All players move forward 1 space.

The United Nations is set up

1941

1945

1945

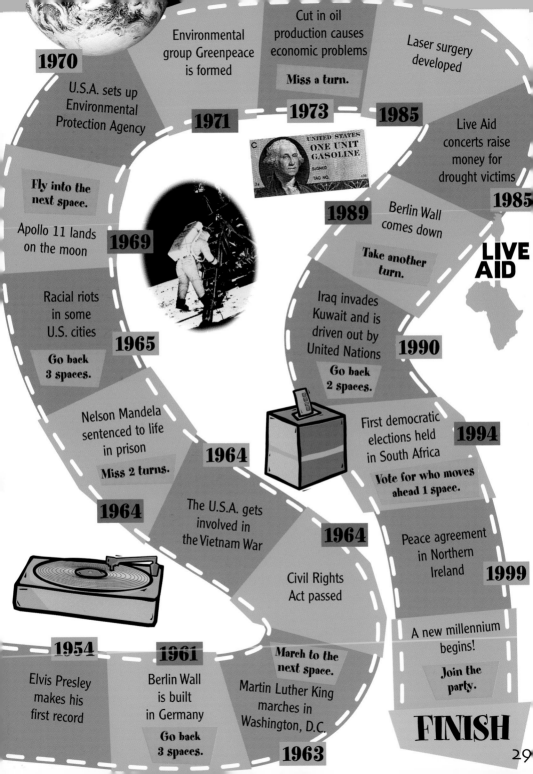

1970

U.S.A. sets up Environmental Protection Agency

Environmental group Greenpeace is formed

1971

Cut in oil production causes economic problems

Miss a turn.

1973

Laser surgery developed

1985

Live Aid concerts raise money for drought victims

1985

LIVE AID

Fly into the next space.

Apollo 11 lands on the moon

1969

Berlin Wall comes down

1989

Take another turn.

Racial riots in some U.S. cities

1965

Go back 3 spaces.

Iraq invades Kuwait and is driven out by United Nations

1990

Go back 2 spaces.

First democratic elections held in South Africa

1994

Vote for who moves ahead 1 space.

Nelson Mandela sentenced to life in prison

Miss 2 turns.

1964

1964

The U.S.A. gets involved in the Vietnam War

1964

Civil Rights Act passed

Peace agreement in Northern Ireland

1999

A new millennium begins!

Join the party.

1954

Elvis Presley makes his first record

1961

Berlin Wall is built in Germany

Go back 3 spaces.

March to the next space.

Martin Luther King marches in Washington, D.C.

1963

FINISH

29

Glossary

alliance – a grouping together for some purpose. Countries that group together during a war are allies.

civil rights – the freedoms and rights that a person may have as a member of a community. Civil rights include the right to fair and equal treatment of all people in the community.

communist – a system of government in which the government owns all the factories and natural resources and controls the production of goods

democratic – working by the rules of democracy, a form of government in which the people vote for their leaders

dictatorship – a country governed by a ruler who has total control

New Deal – the political program of President Franklin D. Roosevelt to make life better during the 1930s

oil crisis – a shortage of oil due to a large increase in the price of oil being sold by OPEC (Organization of Petroleum Exporting Countries). As the price of oil went up, business slowed down because people had less money to spend.

stock market – a market in which shares of ownership in companies are bought and sold. A stock market crash happened when prices for shares dropped suddenly. The shares were suddenly worth much less than what people had paid for them.

United Nations – an organization founded in 1945 to provide a meeting place where countries could settle their differences peacefully. Today, more than 185 countries are in the United Nations.

Index

airplanes	4, 6–7, 28
cars	6–7, 10, 17, 23
civil rights	18, 29
communism	9, 23, 29
computers	4–5, 24–25
dictatorships	13
electricity	6
environment	20–21, 29
Great Depression	12, 28
industry	6, 10, 20
King, Martin Luther	18, 29
Mandela, Nelson	24–25, 29
money	10–12, 17, 22–23
penicillin	11, 28
Presley, Elvis	17, 29
radio	4, 6, 10
space	4, 19, 29
stock market	12, 28
television	5, 16–17, 24
United Nations	15, 26, 28
wars	5, 8–11, 14–16, 19, 28–29
women's rights	9, 18, 28

Research Starters

1 What are some of the changes your family members have lived through over the twentieth century? Interview your family about some of the changes they have seen.

2 Research more about the history of your town, city, or country over the twentieth century. What were some important dates in your area?

3 Choose one decade of the twentieth century before you were born. How would your life have been different if you were born in that decade?

4 Although we often think of the twentieth century as starting in 1900 and lasting through 1999, this is not correct by the calendar system we use today. Our system counts years from A.D. 1—there was no year 0. Celebrating the turn of the century and a new millennium on January 1, 2000, was actually a year early because it was celebrating at the beginning of the old ones' final year.
What do you think about this?